But God!
Family Stories
II

Phyllis E. Griffin

Sources of scriptures are quoted from:

"Access Your Bible from Anywhere."

BibleGateway.Com: A Searchable Online Bible in over 150 Versions and 50 Languages. www.biblegateway.com/

Introduction

This book is dedicated to my family and extended family and is inspired by God's Holy Spirit. It is written to show God's willingness and faithfulness to show up in the lives of everyday people. It is also written to reveal how God manifests himself in various situations or circumstances when we dare to believe or invite him in. The book focuses primarily on three areas. They are God's Miraculous Provision, God's Divine Intervention, and God's Divine Protection. Most of us at some time or another have used the expression, "But God." It is usually said in response to some situation that could have turned out in a totally different way (usually negative or devastating). Believers and nonbelievers alike have had these types of experiences and situations. In this book, my goal is to magnify the power of God at work in each story, situation, and experience. It is my prayer that the stories help people see how approachable and loving our Heavenly Father is. I also hope each story will speak to the hearts of every reader and draw them closer to God. May every reader realize and know that whatever God did for the individuals in this book, he is able and willing to do the same thing for them.

Disclaimer

The following testimonies are real people and events. Permission was granted by each individual and names may be altered to protect the privacy of each party.

Table of Content

God's Miraculous Power & Provision   pg. 6

God's Divine Protection   pg. 20

God's Divine Intervention   pg. 36

God's Miraculous Power & Provision

A Clothing Miracle

Having gone to visit her aunt in the winter of 1985, Elaine took a reasonable amount of clothing with her. It was a cold wintry day snowing in fact when she boarded the huge greyhound bus. She didn't really have a plan or schedule as to how long she would be visiting her aunt, but she just knew she needed to get away from her current circumstance. She was young, single, but most importantly she was embracing her quest for a more intimate relationship with God. She longed to know him better and how to exercise her faith more effectively in him. It was for those reasons and the pursuit of God's will that compelled her to leave her hometown and visit her aunt in Little Rock, Arkansas.

Upon arriving there, she hunkered down in the back bedroom of her Aunt Bob and Uncle Mike's quaint and cozy house. They welcomed her with open arms which was truly a blessing. This was both a serious and pivotal time in her life, and she needed a place where she could seek God without distractions. She had so many questions and needed so many precise answers. She desperately wanted to know the will of God for her life and wanted to live it out. It was there that her life would change FOREVER. It was there that she experienced God responding to her prayers in very unique ways. For instance, though she had brought a reasonable amount of clothing with her, she still needed and desired more.

In particular, she desired to have more dresses and skirt outfits to wear to church. So, she prayed about it, and low and behold, one day something miraculous happened! While she was praying in the bedroom closet, something fell down from the top of the closet. Of course, when it fell, it startled her. She thought, "What in the world was that?" So, she opened the door so she could see what had fallen, and to her surprise, it was a bag of clothes. YES! Nice, nice clothes! It was a bag of dresses, skirts, and jackets. The outfits were stuffed in the bag, and they were just the right size for her. What a wonderful and precise blessing! God is so good. Later she spoke to her aunt about the clothing, she did not know how they had gotten there. She could only speculate that they might have been put there by her son or his girlfriend which she had not seen in years. However they had gotten there, Elaine only knew that God had answered her prayer! The clothing had been placed there perhaps years earlier, and they became a MIRACULOUS answer to her prayer. Through that experience, she felt even closer to God. She also felt confident that he was very much aware of her and her circumstances. The experience also encouraged her faith that God would reveal his will for her life and give her the answers that she so desperately needed.

"Ask, and it shall be given you; seek, and ye shall find; knock, and it shall be opened unto you" Matthew 7:7 (KJV)

Homeschooling-A Perfect Fit

Being disappointed with her high school and public education experience, Chel decided to take a different route with her own children. She, being more technical and artsy minded, found it very hard to attend schools that offered very little to nurture or develop both her passions and interests in school. She also found it amiss and a bit insulting that the history of her own culture was vaguely taught or celebrated. She wanted and desired her children to have a more truthful and rich understanding of their own culture and where they originated from. She wanted them to know and understand their origin from their literal geographics to their grandmama's kitchen table. She needed them to know and understand their heritage coming directly from her lips of clay into their inquisitive minds and keen ears. So, after having her three sons, she set out on her personal journey of homeschooling. A journey she hoped would be beneficial for her sons not only intellectually and educationally, but also wholly. That is to say, she wanted them to benefit and be affected in a positive way in every aspect of their lives. This journey began with some definite trial and error experiences while she navigated through and researched a variety of curriculums. She also researched a variety of homeschooling models, and schools that were successful in developing their students not only in academics, but also in teaching them core disciplines primarily through their interests.

Finland was one of the resources that she researched. After doing her research, she decided to adopt some of their ideas because of their teaching models and student success. In Finland's model, they uniquely grouped students based on their strongest area of disciplines or core subjects. Also, as part of their model, they promoted student interests and community, which was a big win for her. This aspect greatly appealed to her because she knew the importance of nurturing student interests, and she also knew the deficit which comes as a result of failing to. Therefore, she felt that her children could definitely benefit from these key components. The Finland model also strongly promoted both a sense of belongingness and a sense of accountability.

Another reason Chel decided to take the route of homeschooling is because there were some occasional bumps in the road regarding some of the challenges her sons faced in public school. One of her sons, for example, had ADHD and he needed a learning environment that allowed him to be able to be active and move around to meet his kinesthetic needs. While another son was later found diagnosed with having dyslexia, he needed teachers or skilled educators that were trained to directly meet his learning needs. When those educational needs were not met or identified, problems such as behavioral and labeling ensued. You can imagine the frustration that both her sons and her felt. Nevertheless, this further fueled her desire to take on the role as a homeschool mom or homeschool educator. It was indeed a tall order, but she was willing to do it. She was truly willing to fight each day for the success of her sons! In doing so, she also had to fight against the fear of failure! She in no way wanted to fail her sons in their education or in any other way for that matter. In fact, in her mind, FAILURE was not an option! She marched forward to accomplish her mission armed with personal knowledge of her children, their educational needs, and research. She also solicited and coveted collaboration with other homeschooler parents and knowledgeable advocates. With this information and support, she was able to develop individual successful plans that were suitable for her three sons. Her plans included working year-round on their educational goals. They took many, many educational field trips to countless places. They also did a lot of hands-on projects or project-based learning. Chel, the homeschool educator, made it a point to appeal to each of her son's interests and strengths, and also made learning (education) fun.

Long story short, she began her homeschool educational journey with her first son, Rajon. He went on to graduate extremely early and became certified to teach English. As a result, he went to China and taught English for a year and afterwards joined the Air Force working in Intelligence. The second son, Darious, graduated and received certification as a Yoga Instructor and is now working in management for Lowe's. The third son, Samuel, graduated and enrolled in college in California and has received certification in forklifting and is currently employed at the airport.

As a young mother, Chel faced the high calling and challenge of educating her three sons. She also faced the fear of failure, but she PERSEVERED. Today, she is able to share her story of both passion and determination. This is a But God story because she knows that someone much bigger than herself was there to help her through the journey. That someone kept pushing her forward, and constantly spoke these powerful words in her ears, "FAILURE is NOT an OPTION!"

"If any of you lack wisdom, let him ask of God, that giveth to all men liberally, and upbraideth not; and it shall be given him." James 1:5 (KJV)

A Home for the Family

      It was one Saturday in the spring that Willie began to strongly encourage his wife, Phyllis, to get out of the house and go to the mall. That particular day she really didn't want to get out, but reluctantly she did. They both had been praying and decreeing the word of God about purchasing a home for their family. They had experienced apartment living and were presently living in a two-bedroom rental house. Now they were ready to stretch their faith for a home of their own. Who would have known that a simple trip to the mall would prove to be significant to their request. Phyllis got dressed that day and headed to the mall. Before she could get in the door completely, she was met by a familiar smiling face. That smiling face belonged to one of her son's elementary teachers, and she said, "Want to buy a house?" Immediately, she was taken aback and was shocked. She thought to herself, "Of course, I want to buy a house! That's what we've been praying for." A big smile stretched across her face and her heart beat rapidly. She thought could this really be happening? She was filled with both excitement and wonderment. Though she wanted to buy a house and see this dream come true for her family, she did have some normal reservations. She wasn't quite sure about their credit or if it was good enough. However, she didn't let her reservations hinder the defining moment. She didn't let on at all because out of her mouth came the word,

"Yes." With that one word, the process of buying a home for their family began. She started to fill out paperwork and give information at the booth that was set up at the entrance of the mall. After completing the necessary documents and answering questions, the process continued with calls and more information gathering. Soon the process moved to the actual house hunting or searching which meant that their credit was good enough. What a wonderful blessing! They looked at a couple of houses, but in their hearts, they knew which one was right for them. When viewing it, right in the doorway of the master bathroom their hearts were won. They knew within themselves that it was the one for them and their family. In fact, it was exactly what they had prayed for. They had prayed for a three-bedroom home with two bathrooms. Another thing they wanted was a fenced backyard for their children. This particular house had a huge, fenced backyard and was also in a good and quiet neighborhood. Choosing it also meant that their children could continue to attend the same school which was huge for them. All of these things were very important to them, and they felt so blessed that God had heard and answered their prayers. When it came time for closing, they also experienced two more amazing blessings. They found out that their mortgage payment would only be a few dollars more than what they had previously paid in rent. How amazing! They also received a check for the amount of their good faith or earnest money back because they were veterans. By taking this step of faith, God provided for them what they had asked for. They were specific in their request, and they received it! Today, they know that God will bless you when you dare to believe, and he will provide for you whatever you request or need.

"But my God shall supply all your need according to his riches in glory by Christ Jesus." Philippians 4:19 (KJV)

From Skateboarding to a Mazda 3

Bobby Bohanon is a sensible, mild mannered young man who isn't much on confrontation. He loves the tranquility of quietness, unity, and understanding. He is shy by nature but never ever underestimates the brilliancy of his mind, his creativity, or the depth of his innate wisdom (for he is wise beyond his years).

He accomplished the task of graduating high school and entered into the workforce. He was fortunate to land a job which was right down the street from his house. He enjoyed skateboarding back and forth to work. It was exciting. It was cool. It was the 'in' thing to do. However, as with many things, the season for that mode of transportation came to an end. Now it was time for him to have a vehicle, and one that he could call his own. To meet his need, his parents pooled their finances together and purchased him a vehicle. It was a 2004 Dodge Ram truck, and the color was silver. Needless to say, he was 'over the moon' and exceedingly grateful! This gift of transportation gave him a sense of confidence and put a pep in his step. It also encouraged him and made him feel like he could move forward in his life. With that need met, he could get to work without worrying about the elements, especially the uncertainties of the ever-changing weather of Oklahoma. As time went on, things started to go wrong with his truck, but he would work on each issue one by one. He was determined to take care of it and fix whatever needed fixed. As time progressed, major trouble erupted with the vehicle. The engine locked up. Now you know that is major. He ended up putting it in the shop, and the price tag was enormous. It was a whopping $2500.00! That was indeed a hard pill to swallow, and it deeply saddened him. However, despite the price tag, he was determined not to let it go. He wanted to hold on to it like a treasured possession. He was equally determined to find a way to get it out of the shop. By some miracle, determination, and strategy, he believed this would happen. So little by little he and his mother, Shamika, made payments on the said amount. For seven to eight months, he was without his 'beloved silver Dodge Ram.' Finally, one day his mother showed up at the shop and handed them the final payment. She picked the vehicle up and brought it to him. When he saw it, he cried tears of gratitude! He was so grateful to have his truck back, and immediately, he could breathe a sigh of relief. Unfortunately, his excitement and relief were relatively short-lived. After getting it back, the truck started overheating. By this time, he had moved out and was living on his own. The overheating nightmare kept happening repeatedly. Again and again, he faced this reoccurring, frustrating situation. It was like tearing and burning a hole in his soul. As a result, he found himself walking back and forth to work again and eventually, he lost his job. If that was not enough, depression swooped in and sat on him like a ton of bricks, but somehow, he made it through it. Then the vehicle was towed to the shop yet another time, for the same thing and he and his mother met with the owners. They did not say a lot initially, though they were visibly upset and fed up. But then the moment came when his mother spoke up like a mama bear defending her cub with tears streaming down her cheeks. Tears of hot anger and frustration in fact. She communicated bravely and aired both their grievances and disappointments respectfully. Despite her efforts, there would be no favorable resolve in this matter, But God. This forced them into a situation where they had to trust God and look for another vehicle. So, they did.

Bobby and his mother started their search for another vehicle with grit and determination. They went to a dealership in Norman, Oklahoma where he saw a Mustang that he really liked. However, after completing the application process, he was turned down. Needless to say, he was disappointed and upset. The thought loomed in both their minds if he was really turned down for the reason that was given or was it sheer prejudice. Surely, they would never know the answer, but things just didn't seem right in that situation. Despite the letdown, they continued to move forward. They had an objective and a goal and were determined to get the desired results. They talked about it and decided to wait for a while for the right door to open. After waiting for a time, they felt led to go to a dealership in their hometown, Lawton, Oklahoma. When they did, they found that it was the place of favor for their miracle. They went through the application process there. It showed that Bobby had a terrific credit score, but he had little on his credit history profile. However, with help from his mother he was approved to get a trustworthy and reliable vehicle. It was a 2019 Mazda 3. Glory to God! He was excited, grateful, and thankful all at the same time. He knew that God had made a way for him. Until this very day, he also thanks his mother for helping him reach his goal of being a vehicle owner of a reliable and dependable vehicle.

"And God is able to make all grace abound toward you." II Corinthians 9:8 (KJV)

The Journey to Journeyman

We've all heard the saying, 'We plan but God unplans.' Sometimes in the simplest circumstance our plans can be interrupted, changed, or even redirected. For instance, plans to go to a particular store may be stopped by other situations arising. The same plans may be delayed because of some other unforeseen mishap. In the same way, plans to visit a relative can be put on hold for another time, rescheduled, or altogether canceled because of some catastrophic event. The truth is we don't always know why our plans don't go the way we plan, or the way we want them to. However, we can trust that there is an unseen force at work behind the scenes. We can also trust that somehow things seem to work out as they should for our lives by God's grace. I personally believe that the unseen or invisible force is God at work because he knows what he has designed us for. Or, we could say that he definitely knows what his purpose is for our lives. He has designed each of us both specifically and uniquely to accomplish certain things or tasks. Let's see how his plans unfolded in the life of John who is fondly called Junior.

John had every intention of becoming a nurse, but God had other plans. How wonderful it would have been for him to follow in the footsteps of his father, John Sr., who was both an EMT and an RN for many, many years. Or, how honorable it would have been for him to follow after his grandmother, Delois, who was an LPN for at least two decades. However, when it comes to God's plans, sometimes he sets our feet on a totally different path. That's because he wants to fulfill his plan for us which is not necessarily the same plans of our parents or our grandparents. So, we could definitely say that sometimes God unplans our plans in order to accomplish something different in us and through us. We find this to be true in the life of John. He had worked and received his license for plumbing and had worked in the field for quite a period of time. He enjoyed learning the ins and outs of the trade. He also enjoyed having the opportunity to meet the needs of so many people. He especially liked extending his hands to help the disadvantaged and the elderly.

However, in 2003, he started college through a tuition reimbursement program on his job. Though he had a mind to go into nursing, a woman in human resources planted a pivotal seed into his mind and heart. The seed was planted when she told him that the company needed an ELECTRICIAN. It was like hearing the Macedonian call for help for him. It was at that point that his plans changed. Or, we could say that God unplanned his plans or changed them. As a result, he decided to declare his major in Industrial Electricity. By God's grace and with his sheer determination, he completed the program with flying colors! This opened the door for him to work in the electrical field for the company and later for other companies. During his career, he has worked in different capacities such as maintenance, industry, and as an apprentice. He has also endeavored to grow his own business as an apprentice. He has worked diligently and has continued to hone his skills and learn more and more of the ins and outs of the field.

In 2014, he was graced to land a job at Tyson's Food as an Automation Technician. He has enjoyed the work there and continues to learn and thrive. It has been both fulfilling and rewarding to him and given him the capacity to grow.

John had another thing that he wanted to accomplish in the electrical field. He wanted to become certified as a residential journeyman. That desire tugged at his heart for many years though sometimes it seemed far away. However, he never let it go. He held onto it with bulldog faith and determination. Eventually, in September of 2023, his desire and dream were realized at the handsome age of 55 years old. He took the state certification exam for residential journeyman and passed it. Mission accomplished and goal completed! John is a good example of what perseverance, determination, and hard work is able to accomplish. He is also a perfect example of how God will sometimes unplan our plans, and he will lead us into his plans. If God does that, it is always going to be for our good. It is always going to be for what he has designed us for. We just need to learn to trust the plan, which is to say, trust God's plan. For his plans, will always yield the best results or outcomes in our lives.

"A man's heart deviseth his way: but the LORD directeth his steps."
Proverbs 16:9 (KJV)

God's Divine Protection

The Name of Jesus Foils the Enemy's Murderous Plan

What started off to be a typical Saturday ended up being anything but. Phyllis' plans for that day were to meet up with some friends and have lunch. They always enjoyed one another's company and had a great deal in common. So, meeting for lunch was something they all looked forward to. They had decided to meet at twelve o'clock, so she prepared to go. They had chosen to eat at the mall where there would be few people. They chose it because many of the stores was closed. They also knew they would be able to spread out to protect themselves because they were still in the Covid-19 (Corona) pandemic.

Phyllis left home a few minutes before twelve not knowing the terror that was ahead. She did what she always did, and she drove as she always did to get to her destination. As she left her home, she turned onto Country Club Road and proceeded to the light. When she made it to the light, she looked both ways as we all were taught to do, and the traffic was clear. So, she made a right hand turn onto a well-traveled road called the Shawnee Bypass. After checking to see if everything was clear, she then signaled and got into the left lane. Unbeknownst to her, terror, anger, and the spirit of murder would confront her that day on that road. As she was driving, she caught a slight glimpse of a vehicle behind her which swiftly moved to the right side of her vehicle. She had her window rolled down, her music was playing, and she was just minding her own business. Then, she looked to her right side again and saw a Caucasian man in a big black truck. He had fierce anger written all over his face, and he was spewing out W-O-R-D-S. They were ANGRY, ANGRY WORDS. They were MURDEROUS, RAGING WORDS though they seemed to be inaudible against the music playing in her car. However, his next actions were telltale and would express his MURDEROUS, DARK intentions! All of a sudden, he lifted a gun which looked to be a rifle or a shotgun. The GUN had a long body and had scope on it. The man started pointing the gun at her and continued to spit out his ANGRY, HATEFUL words. She was in shock and could not believe what she was seeing! She quickly moved to the far left lane to get away from him, but then he moved to the lane she had previously been in. He moved like a determined predator who was bent on killing his prey. He continued to lift his weapon and point it at her, and he tried to focus on getting a clear shot. Suddenly the light turned red, and he was still there raging, speaking, and aiming his gun! It seemed like eternity! It seemed like time stood still. Desperate for help she cried out, "Jesus, help me! Jesus, help me!" So many thoughts raced across her mind in those moments. She thought of the possibility of that being her last day on Earth. She thought of her life being ended for some unknown reason and becoming another statistic. She also thought of being shot and her brain being splattered on her steering wheel and all over her car, but WHY? She knew in her heart of hearts that if God didn't intervene her life would be over. The date and time would be August 14, 2021, at approximately twelve noon. She desperately tried to dial 911 but her fingers just seemed to fumble while the light lingered on red seemingly for an infinity! She was nervously unsuccessful, so she made a decision to move whether the light was red or green. Instantly, she sped into oncoming traffic on the opposite side of the road. She made a calculated decision to take her chances. Thankfully, the ongoing traffic was sparse, and no one was positioned in the lane she was headed toward. As she drove into the oncoming traffic, the man also made a turn as if he was going to follow her. Fear set upon her, but she continued to go forward. By God's grace, instead of him following her, he kept straight. She assumed that he went into the Lowe's parking lot, but she wasn't sure. Frantically, she called 911 again and nervously told them what had happened. She was informed that they had already gotten a call about the same person, and they asked if she could pull over and wait for an officer. Her reply was, "No." she said no because she didn't know where the perpetrator was or if he was going to come after her again. So, she gave the 911 dispatcher her home address instead. Before she could get to her house and tell her husband what had happened, the officer was already there.

The officer took the incident report, and she told him as best she could what had happened. He showed her a picture and asked her if that was the man. At that moment, her brain froze, and she couldn't say definitely that that was the person. The traumatic event of that day had caused her brain to go into both survival and protective mode. In other words, she drew a blank! She knew she had seen the man and the intense anger on his face, yet she could not remember what he looked like! That had to be a very difficult place to be. Later that afternoon, the officer returned to her home to let her know that they had the man (the suspect) in custody. Needless to say, it was a great, great relief.

In November of that year, it was time for court, and she was not looking forward to that ordeal. The District Attorney's office had called and talked to her a couple of times prior to the court date. She had to be honest with him about not being able to definitively say, "Yes, this is the man." (Though deep inside, she knew it was him. And, the 911 dispatcher alluded to and gave confirmation that it was him, as well). She prayed that her mind, her memory would be released, but she still drew a blank. Her mind continued to stay in survival and protective mode. So, she had to be honest about it knowing that the perpetrator would probably not be convicted. However, she made the decision to go and face the person in court. She knew she had to do it for herself and for her personal right to be safe, protected, and respected. On the court day, her husband, sons, grandson, and a dear friend, Suzie Buck, came with her. Before court, she asked God to word her mouth and to give her both wisdom and courage. God was faithful and gracious to do just that for which she was thankful.

She took the stand and answered the questions of the District Attorney. She answered each question to the best of her ability. Finally, it was time for her to be questioned by the defense attorney. She steadied herself to answer his questions with both courage and clarity. Then, the defining moment arrived and was inescapable. The moment that she had so dreaded. It was the moment that the question which the whole case hinged upon was finally asked. It was spoken almost with a certain mockery as if he knew what the answer would be. That question was, "Could she identify the man (the perpetrator)? Could she point him out in the courtroom?" With both regret and conviction prevailing in her conscience she said, "No." Shortly after her response both the defense attorney and the district attorney approached the bench and collaborated with the judge. The judge then dismissed the charges, and the perpetrator was let go. You might say, "Well he got off scott free." However, she would venture to say that there is both justice and mercy with God.

After the court session, the district attorney met with Phyllis, her family, and her friend. He shared with them that on that day (August 14, 2021) the man had a huge fight with his wife and a weapon was involved. He left home intending to kill one of his friends and then force police officers to kill him. When they heard this, they were all shocked and baffled, but thankful that God intervened and spared at least four lives that day. The life of the man's wife, his friend's life, the man's life, and the life of Phyllis. Only God has all the answers as to why she was thrown into the mix of the devastating circumstances that day, but one thing she is very sure about. That one thing is that the name of Jesus has power against any murderous spirit, or any weapon formed about one's life. God showed her great mercy that day to which she is so grateful, and she is determined to live every day for his glory.

"For whosoever shall call upon the name of the Lord shall be saved." Roman 10:13 "No weapon that is formed against thee shall prosper." Isaiah 54:17

Wrecked, But Still Alive

Richard and Herb loved the adventures of driving, and I mean driving and riding really, really fast. Even though neither of them owned their own car, they loved the adrenaline that driving and riding produced. Somehow, they, especially Richard, would manage to charm somebody (usually a friend or family member) out of their car and their keys. Most of the time he would use a farce to convince them that he really needed to use their vehicle and was quite skilled at presenting himself trustworthy. For instance, he would say something like, "I need to use your car to take so and so somewhere." These were some of the charming and convincing words that would usually roll off of his tongue. Mind you now, while saying these words, he knew just how to keep a straight and presumably honest face. He would also add something like, "I'll put some gas in the car just to make sure he could seal the deal." Richard was such a kidder back in those days. On the other hand, Herb usually went along for the ride. However, when opportunities arose, he would use some of the very same pretentious lines. He would take off with some unassuming person's vehicle to get his thrill on or his adrenaline rush.

One day Richard put on his charm and asked a neighbor if he could use her car to take his son's mother to the store. The neighbor was so taken with admiration for him wanting to take his girlfriend to the store that she immediately handed over the keys to her beautiful, light blue station wagon. She, being young and naive, took his charm at face value, and she bought his story hook, line, and sinker. After getting the keys, Richard, who was as high as a kite, left. Shortly afterwards, he picked up his brother, Herb. That day they were like two peas in a pod because they were both under the influence of alcohol. Or, shall we say liquor or oil as it was commonly called back in the day. So here you have two men high as a Georgia's pine tree in a borrowed vehicle. One driving and the other revving him on and encouraging him to go as fast as he could. They quickly left the city limits of their hometown, Blytheville, Arkansas and headed to the river. The river (Mississippi) was a place that many, many people frequent to have enjoyable family gatherings and activities. Surprisingly, they made it out there without being stopped by a police officer or having an accident. Thank Goodness! When they got there, no one else was there at the time. Richard then decided to back the car onto a boat ramp only to miss the ramp. The front of the car slipped into the river but thankfully, in spite of their condition, they were able to push it out. Shortly afterwards, they decided to head back to Blytheville. Richard was still at the wheel and still under the influence as well as Herb. On their way back, they were quickly approaching a curve. Approaching them on the two lane highway was a huge, eighteen wheeler truck. When Herb looked up and saw it, fear gripped his heart! He responded by abruptly snatching the steering wheel out of Richard's hands hoping to avoid crashing into the big truck. The car immediately swerved and ended up nose diving into an embankment. Herb's head instantly slammed into the windshield. Thankfully, Richard only had some minor scrapes and bruises along with soreness throughout his body. They were both able to get themselves out of the vehicle, but immediately afterwards arguments ensued. Each one blaming the other. Each one pointing the finger at the other. As for the car, it was later declared to be TOTALED! Briefly after the accident, they were given a ride back to town. It was sometime later that the trusting neighbor was given the bad, bad news. Needless to say, she was beyond upset and in disbelief. However, they made her a sweeping promise. They promised to get her car fixed or repaired if possible. Consequently, she was left only with their promise to hold on to. As for Richard and Herb, they were left with conviction and the sobering reality of the events of that day.

It is plain to see that God spared both Richard and Herb's lives that day though they made some very wrong choices or decisions. What could have ended up being a tragedy in so many ways God chose to show great mercy and intervention. Great are the wonders of God our Father. It is sometimes said that God takes care of babies and the foolish. That day God reached out his protective hand upon these two men and demonstrated his care and constant love. His hand of protection was extended to them not because they were babies or wise, but because God's mercy is daily dispensed to us even when we make foolish or unwise decisions.

"O give thanks unto the LORD; for he is good because his mercy endureth forever." Psalms118:1 (KJV)

Rescued from Power Lines by the Power of God's Grace

    Keith has been a long distance truck driver for many, many years. In fact, it has been his passion for approximately thirty years. He has loved embracing the highways, meeting all kinds of people, as well as, the much needed solitude that his career has afforded him. He has loved taking charge of his destiny and knowing that wherever he goes or wherever he travels God always has his back. He has loved and prided himself in the adrenaline rush that his Big Eighteen Wheelers have given him on the road down through the years. He has had the same CB handle, "Can't Get Right," for decades and is currently enjoying his big Mack truck which he calls, "Seahawk!"

    He has traveled from A to Z places and has encountered, shall we say, a handful of situations. On or about June 1, 2023, he faced a situation which he had never experienced before. While traveling in North Carolina on the state highway, some private contractors were working on power lines for a golf course. They had put up their own electrical pole but failed to put the power lines up to at least 13ft. Several trucks were ahead of him and were able to get past the work area without incident. However, when he approached the area, things changed, and they changed rapidly. Immediately, things became life threatening and hazardous! As Keith approached and tried to go through the work area, the power lines began to get caught on the top of his truck causing two poles to fall and a third one to break. When they did, they started wrapping around his truck. They wrapped around it like a tightly gripped rope or a tightly gripped zip tie. It was indeed a very frightening, jaw dropping experience. He saw it and he also heard the surging of the electricity as the power lines made contact with his truck. For a brief moment, he thought, "This is the end!" When it really registered to him what was happening, he called out, "JESUS, JESUS, JESUS!" This was a call for help to the Almighty God and also a release of his faith! Afterwards, he called 911. The operator said to him, "Don't move and Don't touch anything liquid!" Keith listened attentively to the operator's instructions, but he had another pressing problem. His problem was not only the imminent danger before him, but also his bladder posed a problem because it was Full! He desperately needed to relieve himself. Simultaneously, he was faced with dual EMERGENCIES! One, if he moved, it could have triggered a tragedy. And two, if he relieved himself, he faced the possibility of being ELECTROCUTED! Or, in his words, "I didn't want to be a crispy critter." To say that his situation was extremely urgent is indeed an understatement. Yes, he needed God, and all of the earth advocates available. And so, it was. In a matter of a short time, the fire department, ambulance, state trooper, and the electrical company showed up on the scene. The electrical workers' first priority was to ensure Keith's safety. They worked intensely to kill the power of the power lines that were wrapped around his truck. They worked at a safe distance from the truck to deaden the power lines and were successful. Afterwards, they were able to cut the power lines off the truck, and Keith was able to get out. OH, WHAT A RELIEF IT WAS! After that, he was told to go over to the ambulance where they took his vital signs, and of course, his heart rate was out of whack. Who wouldn't be shaken up after such an ordeal? Whose heart wouldn't be beating erratically? But what did Keith do? He declared himself to be OK. Even though they advised him to go to the hospital repeatedly, he refrained from going. Even after one of the EMTs whispered to him, "If you go to the hospital, you'll never have to work another day in your life." He refused to go, still declaring himself okay! He says he knew in his heart that wasn't the right thing for him to do, so he chose not to do it.

Today, he is still driving his Big Mack, "Seahawk," and is loving life. He says, "Life is for living and we don't have all the time in the world to live it." He is telling his story and sharing his faith as he travels from state to state. He is also sharing the good news about the mercy and the grace of the Almighty God. He knows that things could have ended so much differently had it not been for the intervention of God. Keith knows that he was rescued from those dangerous power lines by the power of God's grace that eventful day.

"In my distress I called upon the Lord and, cried unto my God: he heard my voice out of his temple, and my cry came before him, even into his ears." Psalms 18:6 (KJV)

The Little Rock Tornado

In the spring of 2023, Yvette went to Little Rock, Arkansas for a celebratory event. Traveling with her were two of her daughters, Kaylee and Britta. Also traveling with her were four of her grandchildren. They had gone to Little Rock to celebrate one of her son-in-law's birthdays. They had planned a wonderful surprise for him, the party would start at approximately 6:00 p.m. The venue which they had chosen was a recreational facility.

Before the party started around 4:00 p.m., they were out and about, and it began to lightly sprinkle. Gazing at the sky, they saw some clouds moving about slowly and normally. Nothing about them suggested trouble or any impending danger. However, as they were making their way back to their hotel, something swiftly changed in the clouds and in the weather. The clouds which were earlier moving slowly and normally had begun to move quickly as though they were racing. They were turning and turning and moving and moving so rapidly now. They looked both eerie and alarming. They were gray in color and began to billow. In an instant, the rain went from being a slight sprinkle to a sudden deluge. Yvette said, "It was like heaven opened up and the rain poured and poured down." It beat vehemently on her car, and its windshield. So much so, that as she tried to drive, she could feel the viciousness of every drop. She drove as if by blind faith. She struggled terribly to see what was in front of her, but she kept on driving. Fear gripped her heart and those who were traveling with her. However, her determination to get her family out of harm's way eventually prevailed. She was finally able to get them to a store. Once there, they grabbed whatever they could to cover the children from the vicious rain and hurriedly ran inside the store. Entering the store gave each of them a sense of both relief and safety. In fact, one of Yvette's daughters responded to her feeling of relief by lifting her hands to God and Shouting Out a Prayer. Not long after they arrived inside, the announcement came over the intercom for EVERYONE to Take Cover! Everyone scurried to do exactly that. As they did, they could hear the loudness of the sirens. They continued to sound off and warn of danger Over and Over again for approximately twenty to thirty minutes. Though twenty to thirty minutes may relatively be a short period of time, in that situation, it seemed to last FOREVER! Finally, the all clear announcement was given because the tornado had left that particular area. Now everyone could breathe a sigh of relief and go to their specific destinations. That evening God led Yvette and her family, and all the others that were in the store to a place of safety. He was truly watching over them in the midst of that tornadic storm. He provided a place of refuge and security for them in their time of trouble.

"God is our refuge and strength, a very present help in trouble." Psalms 46:1 (KJV)

A Bout with Cancer

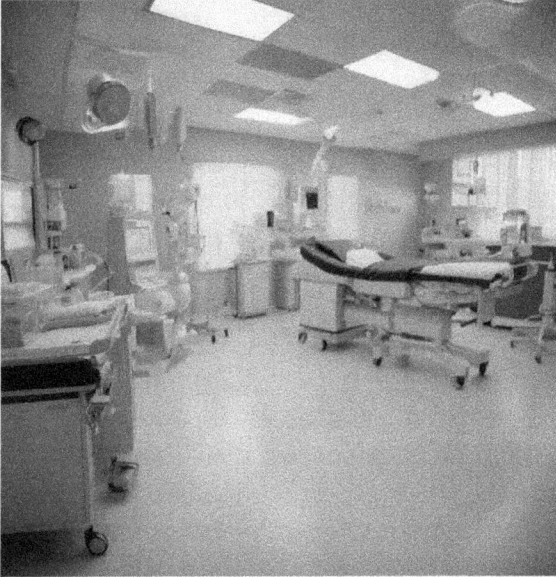

In 2014, Willie was diagnosed with cancer. Anytime the word cancer is heard or used it is NEVER a good thing. The diagnosis came after several years of having routine blood work done and other routine tests ran. One of the tests that was routinely done is called a PSA (which every man should have one annually). PSA stands for Prostate Specific Antigen. PSA is a protein produced by both normal and cancerous cells in the body. The test measures how much PSA is present in the bloodstream. In most cases of prostate cancer, the PSA level increases. The usual or normal range of PSA is normally 3 or below. However, in some cases, even at these levels, cancer can still be present. That is why it is so imperative that men get annual testing and share any abnormal symptoms with their physicians.

For several years, Willie's PSA protein level measured at normal levels. However, after a while, they began to spike or elevate. This caused great alarm and concern for his doctors which led to a biopsy being done. During the biopsy, twelve specimens were taken to be tested. Meanwhile, he and his wife waited in faith. They waited patiently yet experiencing a degree of anxiety. When the call came in, unfortunately, it was not the result or report that they wanted to hear. The report showed that from the biopsy one of the twelve specimens was cancerous. This was definitely ALARMING! However, they still found themselves REJOICING in the

LORD realizing that the report could have been much, much worse. In that, they were truly both thankful and grateful! Why? Because the results could have been that ALL twelve specimens were found to be cancerous. BUT GOD! Yet on the other hand, CANCER is CANCER! No one wants it, not even a little bit of it. Right? So, the battle was ON! At that point, the doctor's medical plan or strategy was to put him under surveillance or simply monitor his PSA levels. His wife to some degree, was left shaking her head and wondering, "Why don't they just take it out?" In her frustration, she even contemplated going to the White House to see President Obama because to her it just didn't make any sense to leave it(cancer)in his body! She wanted her husband to be ALIVE-she wanted her husband to be OKAY. So, realizing she didn't have any control over the doctor's decision, she became proactive with the help of her sons. She started changing her cooking habits and their eating habits, and also became big on juicing. She began to do what she could to bring health and healing to her husband's body. Of course, this was coupled with both of them believing and speaking the word of God. Meanwhile, Willie remained positive and didn't complain about what he was going through. He kept living, working, and preaching the word of God. He kept believing and trusting in the Lord. In his case, he never had any symptoms outside of frequent urination. He didn't take the time to feel sorry for himself, but by God's grace kept taking care of the things that needed to be done. However, inwardly, he struggled from time to time with the question of why. One day God gave him the answer, and God's reply was, "It's only a test." That inspirational word from God gave him confidence, relief, and energy to continue to fight the good fight of FAITH.

As time went on, approximately two years later his PSA level reached over five. This meant that the cancer was growing and becoming more and more life threatening. The chance of it spreading outside the prostate was becoming more probable. Therefore, the doctor then started talking to him about having surgery. He thoughtfully took it under advisement. He and his wife prayed about the situation. Later, after sensing peace and joy from God, our Father, he decided to have the surgery. The specialist that was to do the surgery was located in another city. By the grace of God, he was one of the best in the field. Though they were grateful for that, Willie and his wife, Phyllis, knew that he was in the hands of the very best, The Almighty God.

The surgery was performed in 2016 and was successful by God's grace. The prognosis was favorable, and no chemotherapy or radiation was needed. All Praise and Glory to the Almighty God! Willie encourages every man to have their annual PSA testing done without hesitation, fear, or shame. It is a simple blood test that takes only a few minutes and can literally save your life. It is a tool of early detection which can preserve both your health and ensure longevity. He also warns against allowing misinformation about the effects of prostate cancer or surgery or even male potency, to cause men not to receive testing. The survival rate from early detection of prostate cancer is tremendously high and male potency is both sustainable and achievable. Willie has been graced to be a cancer survivor and has enjoyed his life since facing this challenging experience. Prostate cancer can kill, but God can bring healing and restoration both supernaturally and through early detection. God protected and extended Willie's life, and he continues to give him praise and glory.

"But God has helped me to this very day; so I stand here and testify to small and great alike." Acts 26:22 (NIV)

God's Divine's Intervention

A Revealing Dream

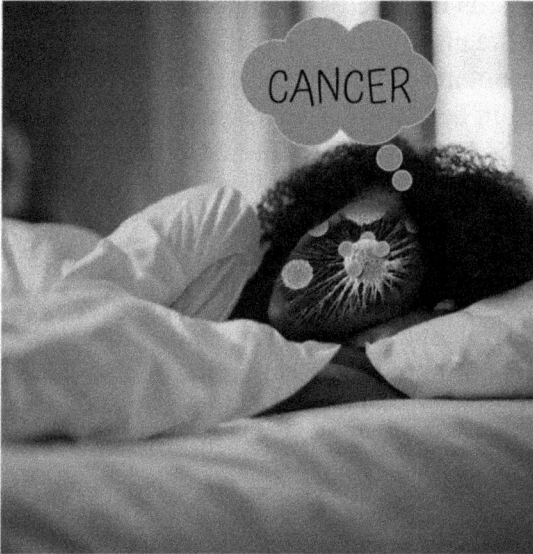

In the early 1980's Carol, a certified nurse's assistant, had a peculiar yet informative dream. The dream was both disturbing and quite revealing. In her dream, she saw herself having a diagnosis of cancer. Not only did the dream reveal that she had cancer, but she was also shown what type of cancer it was. The type of cancer which was revealed in the dream was cervical cancer. Cervical cancer is cancer that starts in the cells of the cervix. It develops slowly over time and can present with little or no symptoms in the early stages. In the advanced stages of cervical cancer, abnormal discharge or vaginal bleeding may be experienced along with pain in the pelvis, fatigue, weight loss, or nausea. This is why it is so imperative for women to have annual exams called pap tests (or Pap smear) or HPV tests. This type of cancer is often referred to as the 'silent killer.'

Carol shared her dream with several family members and a few other people, as well. When she went to the doctor, the truthfulness of the dream was put to the test. Did she really have cervical cancer or was this merely a dream? The truth undoubtedly had to come out. It had to be revealed. She and her family waited nervously for the test results. When they came back, the dream was confirmed. Its authenticity was absolute. It was true. It was real. During her visit with the doctor, he spoke about the seriousness of the diagnosis or condition. However, unbeknownst to him, even though his words were sobering, they were not new news. Surprisingly, his words rendered a strange calming effect while solidifying the validity of her dream. By some invisible power, his words of confirmation were not able to make her desperately afraid. Why was that? It was because within her dream she sensed a confidence and an assurance that she was going to be alright. She knew God had given her the dream to show her what was going on in her body. He wanted to prepare her for both the diagnosis and the surgery. He also wanted to deposit within her spirit faith and assurance.

After the doctor's diagnosis, she was scheduled for surgery. The surgery went very well, and the doctor was able to successfully remove all of the cancer. When the surgery was over, the doctor shared with her the descriptive formation of the cancer. It was found to be in a cluster in the cervix, and it was also confined to that specific area. This was indeed good news! She and her family could exhale now. They could breathe a sigh of relief!

Amazingly, in her case, she did not have to have chemotherapy or radiation which is somewhat rare. However, this was exactly what God had shown her in the dream. Praise and Glory to God! From that time on, she knew within herself that she was going to be alright. What a glorious report! By the grace and goodness of God, Carol has never had another bout with cancer. This testifies of God's unfailing word, his compassion, and his grace. This was truly a, But God dream which led to a But God healing miracle!

"For God does speak- now one way, now another- though no one perceives it. In a dream, in a vision of the night, when deep sleep falls on people as they slumber in their beds." Job 33:14,15 (NIV)

Three Threatening Surgeries

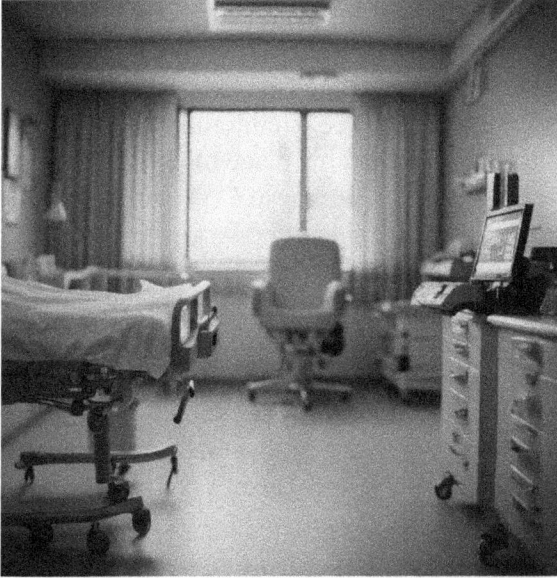

As a young woman, Shamika began having some serious physical problems. Like the woman in the bible, her physical problems and complications involved an issue of blood. Drinking a simple glass of anything would usually leave her clothing soiled. Not just that, but her body was also often riddled with excruciating pain as she went through the frequent bouts of near hemorrhaging. Finally, a visit to the doctor landed her scheduled to undergo a procedure called ovulation (removal of uterus wall lining) to try to resolve the problem. At that point, she wanted the pain to STOP and of course, the issue of blood. She was hopeful that the procedure would bring it all to an end. This was her surgery number one. However, about a year after the procedure, she found herself back at the doctor's office because of some ongoing complications. Nothing had changed much and sometimes it seemed things had gotten even worse. This time the same doctor recommended that she have a partial hysterectomy because an ultrasound revealed she had an ovarian cyst. In the partial hysterectomy, her left ovary would remain intact. Still, what a devastating blow to hear such a recommendation! She was only twenty-nine years old. So, she thought about it and prayed about it then agreed to go through with the surgery. Her goal again was to get rid of both the unbearable pain and the root of the problem. Her second surgery was scheduled in 2009. She went into surgery for the partial hysterectomy, but something happened entry immediately after the doctor began. After making an incision in the initial place of entrance, he saw that the area was profoundly thick because of previous complex scarring. Therefore, he could not continue or complete the operation through that entrance. He literally had to stop the surgery. He then quickly shifted and changed his place of entry to her abdomen. His incision into her abdomen was similar to C-section or what is commonly called a Cesarean. A C-section is commonly performed on pregnant women which is a widely used option to vaginal births. Shamika was well familiar with this type of operation because she had had two of them in the delivery of her two children, Brittany and Bobby. The surgery went well by most accounts and things seemed to be going alright.

Then came 2012, Shamika was met with even more complications. This time the pain that riddled through her body brought her to her bending knees at some point. She was bowled over and she also found herself crawling around on the floor. Tears filled her eyes and rushed down her face because of the terrible and excruciating pain. She went to the doctor once again and this time the doctor wanted to remove her left ovary. Now she was looking at a third surgery, which would leave her with no reproductive organs. What a painful punch in the gut! However, she decided to go for it knowing she absolutely could not go on this way. This time once the doctor got her into the surgery, he discovered that she had an abdominal obstruction. Not only that, he also found that some of her internal organs were matted or twisted together and some had even shifted. For example, her appendix had shifted to the left side of her body and consequently, it was removed during the surgery. The surgery as a whole, though lengthy, was successful and now she is enjoying a much better quality of life.

Through each of these life threatening situations, God's hand was truly upon her. Since the surgeries, some people have said to her, "I don't see how you are alive!" But Shamika knows that it was God looking out for her. She is thankful for the mercy he has shown her through such difficult and challenging times. She gives him the praise because she knows if it had not been for him her prognosis or outcome could have been much, much different.

"He sent his word and healed them." Psalm 107:20 (KJV)

Surviving a Mysterious Condition

In 2017, the day after Thanksgiving, our house phone rang. Though I was still up, cleaning and so forth, I knew that any phone call at that hour (approximately 2:35 am) could not be a good one. I hit the off button on the vacuum cleaner and listened to the message from a friend of both my husbands and mines. The friend said that he was told that my brother, Herb, had possibly been poisoned and was being taken to the hospital. I had been praying prior to the call (it's amazing how God prepares you), so I continued to pray and declare life over him. I felt an unusual peace come over me and knew of God's faithfulness. I began to change clothes and get ready to go to the hospital. My husband was sound asleep, and I didn't want to wake him because I knew this was a case for God. I also knew it was between him and I. So, I headed to the hospital continuing in prayer and speaking words of faith. I almost felt like I was in a daze or dream as I made my way there. Upon arrival, I inquired about my brother and the receptionist confirmed that he was in fact there. She directed me into another room to wait for the doctor. Meanwhile, I met a woman who was a friend of my brother. She had blood over her eyebrow, arm, and her clothes. Though it was our first time meeting, she began to spill out the events that had occurred with my brother. She told me how he had gone somewhere earlier and when he returned, he had a soda bottle, but she was sure that it did not contain soda. He started drinking it and then began sweating profusely. He went to the bathroom and had asked her to get him a wet towel to put on the back of his neck. When she returned back to the bathroom, he was on the floor and was vomiting blood profusely! His eyes started to roll back in his head and then he stopped breathing! The ambulance was called, and when he arrived at the hospital, he was given two pints of blood and fluids to maintain his blood pressure.

Finally, the doctor came out to talk to us. He stated that he suspected that the veins in his throat were ruptured and bleeding. They were preparing to airlift him to a nearby city which was better equipped to help him. We asked if we could go in to see him, and we were not allowed because of the severity of his condition. Shortly thereafter, they were loading him to be taken to the next hospital.

I contacted my sister, Kay, who lived in another town to let her know about the situation. The next day we met at the hospital which Herb had been airlifted to. Thankfully, when we got there, our brother was able to talk to us. He shared with us his frightful and terrible experience after drinking what he thought was soda. He also shared with us that on his way to the hospital, the EMTs kept saying, "He's dying, He's dying!" What a frightening and fear gripping experience!

Today, we are not sure what happened to him. We don't know if he was poisoned or whether the veins in throat ruptured as the doctors had speculated. However, we do know that God granted him an abundance of grace that morning. He spared his life and granted him mercy to walk out of that hospital shortly after that terrifying and life threatening situation. We are thankful that we still have him in our lives today. We are also thankful that God reached out his hand of love and mercy to him that early morning.

"And when I passed by thee, and saw thee polluted in thine own blood, I said unto thee when thou wast in thy blood, Live…" Ezekiel 16:6 (KJV)

Brittany's Emergency Surgery

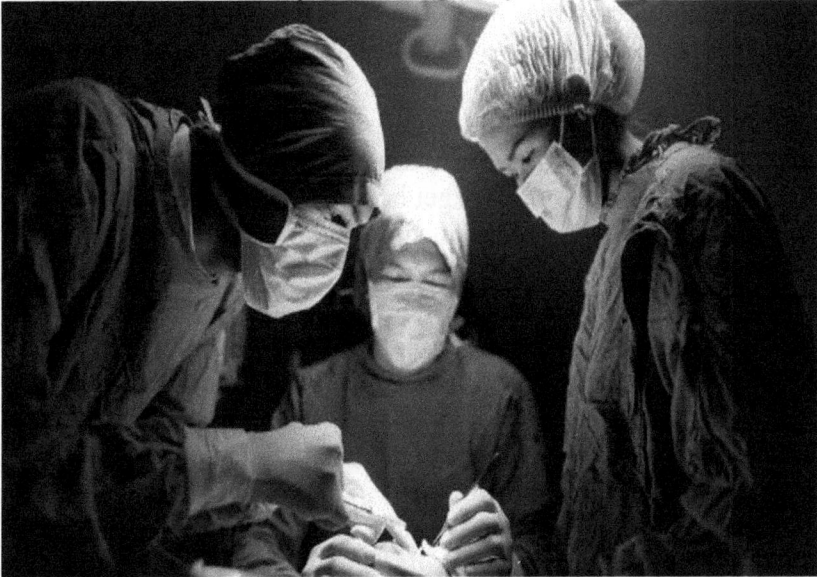

Brittany Bohannon is a very strong and determined young woman. She has pride in the things she has accomplished in life, and always puts her best foot forward when reaching her goals. She is diligent and doesn't mind working hard for the things she wants to obtain in life. In short, she is ambitious, responsible, and quite reliable along with possessing an ever so natural beauty.

As a 25 year old, she has enjoyed the gift of health and being physically fit. However, in the spring of 2023, she experienced something that took her totally by surprise. This experience not only threatened her health but also her life. She had been dealing with some lingering issues with her stomach for a while. So, when she felt some uneasiness in her abdomen, she didn't think it was anything serious or to be alarmed about. The doctor had told her sometime before that she had a case of Gerd Reflux or Acid Reflux. She was on medication for it and things had subsided somewhat, but there were still ongoing issues with it. The medication she was taking gave her some temporary relief, and she was able to go about her daily business and work to some degree. However, that was about to change because another health issue was on the horizon.

One day Brittany began to have sharp, sharp pains in her stomach and in her side. The pain continued so she went to the emergency room only to be sent back home. They didn't find anything wrong to her dismay. The next day or so later, while she was at work, the pain INTENSIFIED. She began to experience sharp pain upon sharp pain in the same two places! So much so, that it became virtually impossible for her to work. The pain became so intense that she could hardly walk and started to faint off. Eventually, somehow, she was able to muster up enough resolve to leave work. She thought if she could just get home and lay down maybe the pain would stop. Well, it didn't! It continued on and on. At this point, she knew she needed to get back to the emergency room. She managed to get to her car, and she drove herself to the hospital. Her abdomen (stomach) was largely swollen, and she looked as though she was a pregnant woman. She was also severely dehydrated and constipated which put added stress on her body. When she got there, they took her vital signs and ran some tests. Shortly thereafter, she was admitted to the hospital and an IV was started. The tests indicated that her appendix was in dire straits. She had appendicitis, and her appendix needed to be removed immediately.

While waiting for surgery, Brittany's mother, Shamika, was careful to share with her what things to expect and shared with her words of assurance. She knew all too well the ins and outs of this type of condition and situation because she had gone through it herself. Amid their heart-to-heart comforting conversations, there was also the doctor's diagnosis and probable speculations. Of course, he had shared the information about the appendicitis, but there was more! The doctor added to the appendicitis diagnosis that it was possible that Brittany's ovaries may also have to be removed. Instantly, her mother said, "No! Don't touch them! Don't touch any of her female organs!" She made this declaration more than once. She was quite adamant about it and left no question about what she meant. She, herself, had gone through the very same thing. Not just the appendicitis, but also the removal of her ovaries at a relatively young age. Having experienced this, she definitely didn't want Brittany to suffer the same thing unnecessarily. It was plain to see that this was definitely an issue of both concern and contention for her mother. Especially since she knew that Brittany didn't have any children yet. Her mother spoke up like a momma bear protecting her cub and made herself perfectly clear concerning the matter. The answer was emphatically, NO!

The time finally came for the surgery and Brittany resigned herself to be at peace. After all, she trusted in the encouraging words of her mother. She also trusted and found solace in the prayers of her family, and of others, which had been said on her behalf. The surgery lasted for three to four hours. During it, it was difficult to find her appendix because of severe scar tissue. When they did find it, it had already ruptured! But God! Needless to say, this caused a great level of concern because of the potential spread of toxins throughout her body. Consequently, a tube was placed in her abdomen to drain off the toxins. If that wasn't enough, her blood pressure was also an issue of concern both before and after surgery. It was extremely elevated which posed a serious danger to her life. They worked immensely to get it under control and to keep it under control.

After the surgery, the doctor shared with them that he hadn't seen anything quite like that before. He also shared that he had never experienced surgery taking that long to remove an appendix. He further said, "She, (referring to Brittany), is blessed to have come through this." The surgery as a whole was successful, and the prognosis was good. At last, Brittany was blessed to get rid of the source of her horrific pain, and she was also able to keep all of her reproductive organs. Praise the Lord! What a wonderful victory! Shortly afterwards, she was released to go home and recuperate for about six weeks. Today, she is back to work and living life. She continues to be thankful for God's grace. She realizes it brought her through such an unexpected and unpredictable health scare.

"Heal me, O Lord, and I shall be healed; save me and I shall be saved: for thou art my praise." Jeremiah 17:14 (KJV)

A Coma, 48 Blood Clots, & Two Black Feet

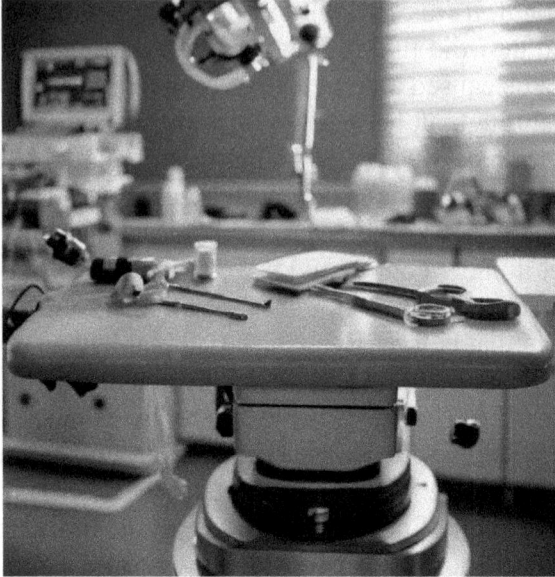

A week before some eventful things happened, Chaplain Dr. Darrell Hartley knew something was wrong. He was so thirsty, parched in fact, like someone stranded in the Sahara Desert. Along with that, he was experiencing frequent urination urges which were highly unusual. Though he knew he was pre-diabetic, these symptoms seem to be way over the top. Besides that, he had a decision to be more proactive concerning his health since learning he was pre-diabetic. Therefore, he thought was keeping a pretty good eye on his dietary intake and habits, and his overall health. However, he would soon find out that serious trouble was lurking ahead. Unfortunately, he was headed for an onslaught of medical complications which were beyond his wildest dreams.

The weekend of July 28th of 2017 would prove to be one of the most trying times of his life. It would not only test his faith but also his wife and those around him. He was at home that weekend and felt like he was dying of thirst. In fact, he would later find out that he was severely dehydrated. He didn't feel well so he laid on the sofa for a bit. Then after a while, he laid on the love seat. Before he knew it, he had passed out. Afterwards, it was a kind of in and out of consciousness that he experienced. The state of being awake and then not being awake which persisted for some time. Thankfully, his wife, Angela, was home, and immediately she knew something was wrong. Something just wasn't right! She took him to the hospital only to find out that he had gone into a diabetic coma. His blood sugar level was 1267 and the normal range is between 70-180 (depending on whether a person is fasting or not). Dr. Hartley was in a coma for four or more days. When he was graced to wake up, his wife was right there by his side. With that battle over and won, they could feel a sense of relief. However, the battle for his life and health was not over. Now they faced even more critical challenges and decisions. If the coma scare wasn't enough, now both of Dr. Harley's feet were BLACK because of the lack of blood circulation. From his toes up to his calves, there were serious complications and definite reasons for alarm. There was also the looming speculation or concern that gangrene had set up in his feet and legs. The doctors ran tests and discovered that he had DVT's. DVTs are Deep Vein Thrombosis. They are blood clots in deep veins, usually in the legs, thighs, or pelvis, and can also occur in the arms. They are dangerous because they block the blood flow into the veins and into the arteries. If they are not removed, they can also break away into other areas of the body such as the lungs and brain and become fatal. So, this was a very serious issue to say the least. Dr. Hartley didn't just have one or two blood clots, but he had 48 blood clots! To say that the prognosis was not good would be a mere understatement. He was told that if they (DVT's) were not removed his legs would have to be amputated. It was like someone knocking all the air out of his lungs and throat. When he heard those words, he cried, and his wife comforted him with a warm embracing hug. In that moment, she became his earthly guardian angel. She was his advocate, source of strength, and support, second to God only. She was there to help him navigate through these critical situations. She was there to help him make the right decisions which would yield favorable results. Finally, he made the decision to have the surgery, and to trust God for the outcome.

The doctors scheduled the surgery and the staff ensured that all the preparatory procedures were done, and protocols were followed. Their objective was to remove as many of the blood clots (DVT's) as possible. Undoubtedly, this would be a difficult operation, but God would be there to guide the surgeon's hand through every precise step. By God's grace, the doctors were successful in removing the DVT's. This allowed blood to circulate throughout both his legs and his feet thereby saving them. What a wonderful blessing to see his natural brown color return to his feet. Praise the Lord! Dr. Hartley had come through the surgery and now his progress was evident. His prognosis was much, much better than before. However, there was still one more hurdle to overcome. In fact, his total recovery was contingent upon it. That hurdle was that he had to be willing to go through both physical and occupational therapy. Without it, amputation was still possible, and atrophy was certain. So, he had to steady his mind and be determined to do whatever it took to regain his health. Again, his wife was right there to cheer him on and to render support. So, the very next day after surgery the therapists showed up! He couldn't believe they were there so soon after surgery, but they were. Against all odds and in spite of the traumatizing pain cascading through his body, he knew what he had to do. Reluctantly, he struggled and strained to get out of his bed, and he started his journey to recovery. It was extremely painful, but he held in the forefront of his mind what would happen if he didn't do it. Step by step and day by day he made his way to recovery. Also, through the process of his recovery, he changed his diet even more and lost approximately 122 pounds.

Today, he is enjoying his life, his wife, and his family. He travels throughout the states helping Veterans in a variety of ways. God brought him through an onslaught of medical complications. He brought him through a diabetic coma, 48 DVT's, and two black feet which could have resulted in amputation. But God! It's plain to see that the enemy wanted to take away his health and or snuff out his life, but God granted him abundant grace. What a wonderful God we serve!

"But I will restore you to health and heal your wounds, declares the LORD." Jeremiah 30:17 (NIV)

K-Mart, A Place of Healing

One day in the early 1990's Phyllis was prompted to go to K-Mart in the town she lived in. At the time, she was living in Muskogee, Oklahoma. The K-Mart in her city had a restaurant inside of it which was located at the back of the store. She enjoyed eating there from time to time and especially enjoyed their grilled chicken sandwiches.

After getting to the store, she made her way to the restaurant area and took a seat. She had no idea what was getting ready to happen to her and how impactful the visit would be, but God did. In fact, she would later realize that it was a divine appointment with the Father. It was a divine set up to meet her at the point of her deepest need that day. You see, she and her husband had gone through a difficult time and experience in the ministry. They had worked with other churches before and had served as a pastor previously. Now they were working with a denominational church whose pastor lived in another state. They were filling in unofficially I guess you could say and were hopeful to be chosen for the pastorship. To their knowledge, everything seemed to be going pretty good at least on the surface. However, there seemed to be a problem arising from one specific family. This family happened to be one of the main families of the church. One of the members in that particular family seemed to be in direct opposition with them. Her husband would preach, and they would rise up in opposition. Nothing they said or did seemed to satisfy the person. This individual was definitely operating under the spirit of rebellion and defiance. After a time, that person and their inner circle started inviting another minister into the church to conduct services without any warnings or head ups. Apparently, the motivation was to pit one minister against another, to cause strife, and to drive her and her husband out of the church. This was definitely a show of blatant disrespect and dishonor. They knew something was going on, but they didn't know exactly what. Shortly thereafter, 'the behind the door' collusion was revealed. They (the church member, her circle, and family) had together worked with the visiting minister and had talked to the overseer (who lived out of town). Their collaboration and conversations back and forth resulted in the overseer allowing the visiting minister to act as pastor in his stead. It was a surprising 'bombshell' that many in the collusion enjoyed, oh so well. It was like someone snatching the rug from under them, and heaping public humiliation upon them like they were criminals. It was like being ambushed by familiar so-called friends with smiling faces. It's difficult to understand why no one had the decency to meet with them or pull them to the side and let them know that they had chosen the visiting minister. No! They had to hear it and find out when everybody else did. How embarrassing! How humiliating! But, she and her husband, Willie, got the message loud and clear! With that being revealed, they knew that God is love, and he is also peace. Therefore, they made the decision to leave the church because they did not want to hinder the ministry there. However, their hearts were wounded and hurt. They were disappointed to say the least, but their faith in God didn't waver. Though they didn't understand why this had happened, they were still determined to trust in the Lord.

They went on with their day to day living and serving the Lord. Then that fateful day came when Phyllis went to K-Mart. Her thoughts fell on the events of the church situation. Thoughts of why flooded her mind. Thoughts of disappointment and grief filled both her mind and her heart. Coupled with these bombarding thoughts were the awful arrows of rejection that seemed to pierce her soul. Thoughts of not being good enough or not being wanted seemed to whisper its cruelty. At times, she became overcome, even overwhelmed with emotions as she sat in the restaurant and tears streamed down her face. As the tears ran down, she began to hear God say, "I Love You. I Love You. I Love You. I Love You. I Love You…" God by the voice of the Holy Spirit kept repeating the same words over and over again. Countless times he said it. Each time he said it, the words began to break through the hurt, the grief, and the pain. They broke through the sorrow and the disappointment. They even penetrated and destroyed the yoke of rejection. Those three words brought healing to her wounded soul. They brought the spirit of rejection subject to the power of God and his unfailing love. Those three words pulled the arrow of rejection out of her soul that day. She felt such a release and a freedom that only God can give. Phyllis learned through this love meeting with God not to ever equate man with God. In other words, though man may reject you, it has nothing to do with God. God, our Father, has decided to receive us unto himself.

That day she left K-Mart feeling loved by God, her creator. She realized that though she and her husband and may not have been loved, appreciated, or accepted by that particular church that had nothing to do with God and his love for them. And, although disappointments had come, God still had a good plan for she and her husband. She also realized that the power of God's love can never be underestimated. It is real, and it can heal, restore, and revive! She further realizes that, if God can't get his words of love or his expressions of love to you through a human being, he will bring you to an intimate place (like K-Mart) and speak them, to you himself!

"He healeth the broken in heart, and bindeth up their wounds." Psalms 147:3 (KJV)

NO Surgery for My Baby!

    Born to Hope and Norico in 1996 was a handsome baby boy. He weighed a little over five pounds and had straight black hair. He was caramel in color and was a sure delight to his parents. Early on as a newborn, the doctor discovered that their precious son had a hernia in his groin. This was both unexpected and unwanted news. It was definitely hard to hear and difficult to digest. The doctor told them that he wanted to operate to alleviate the problem. This weighed heavily on their minds and hearts. However, his mother responded quickly to the doctor's recommendation. Her words to him were, "NO surgery for my baby! NO surgery for my baby! She was very adamant in her decision and her conviction regarding the situation. How could she allow her little baby to be cut on? How could she allow him to go through this traumatizing experience being so, so young and so, so small. She had made her decision, and she knew just who to take her son to. She said, "I'm going to take him to my doctor. Yes, my doctor, JESUS!"

    Sometime later she took Norico Jr. (affectionately called Bubua) to church, and she requested prayers for him. She shared both what the doctor's diagnosis was and his recommendation. She further shared that she didn't want her child to be cut on. After sharing her request, the minister prayed for healing and for God's divine intervention. Hope and Norico Sr.

believed to see God's hand touch their precious bundle of joy. Hope stood in unwavering faith as they waited to see the manifestation of the prayers that had been prayed.

Shortly afterwards, the day came for the next doctor's appointment. On that visit, the doctor ordered another x-ray to be done. When it was completed, there was a stunning and miraculous surprise. The nurse was astonished at what she saw and could hardly believe her eyes. She hurriedly brought the x-rays in for Hope to see them. She showed and explained how the first x-ray showed a hernia while the second one showed no evidence of a hernia. Norico Jr.'s mother, was elated and extremely thankful to God. The nurse said, "I wonder what happened?" Hope replied, "I guess it went back to the pit of hell!" She knew that prayer and their faith caused the power of God to manifest a supernatural non-surgical miracle! What a mighty God we serve. He is the God that can take you from an unfavorable x-ray to a favorable one by his mighty power.

"But Jesus beheld them, and said unto them, With men this is impossible; but with God all things are possible." Matthews 19:26 (KJV)

The Case of a Burning Car

Jeremiah was visiting a friend in his hometown in December of 2016. About 4:00 a.m., they heard an enormous boom outside! Simultaneously, they looked at each other and said, "What was that?" Of course, they immediately rushed to the door to see what was going on! To their amazement, they saw the reason for the enormous sound. The reason for it was his car. It was on fire and bellowing in flames. The flames were fierce as they eerily gave a colorful light to the darkness that surrounded them. What an unexpected and unbelievable sight to see. A brand new shiny, black Impala was going up in smoke for no apparent reason. It totally caught him off guard and his sense of invulnerability or invincibility seemed to shrink. He stood there gripped with shock and bewilderment. It was surreal to say the least. In the midst of what he was seeing, there arose two burning questions. They were who and why? In short, who had done this despicable thing? And, why had they done it? To his surprise, a neighbor had seen two people near his car shortly before the fire. Unfortunately, they didn't have any specific or detailed description of the individuals. They immediately called 911 when they saw the fiery flames and called the fire department. Jeremiah then called his mother and said, "Momma, my car is on fire!" She replied, "Your car is on FIRE? What happened?" He replied, "I don't know!" Then he began to tell her about hearing the loud BOOM and what happened afterwards. Within a short period of time, both the fire department and police department showed up on the scene. They began an investigation which lasted approximately one month. Unfortunately, the investigation came up empty and justice fled like a guilty dog fleeing from his master. To date, the police department has never found out who committed this ghastly crime though suspicion and leads were generated. However, we do know that God witnessed everything that happened that morning. Therefore, he and his family prayerfully put the situation in his hand. For he has said, "Vengeance is Mine, I will repay."

Through this alarming and eventful situation, they still managed to come away from it with thankfulness to God. They were thankful because they knew that this story could have ended so differently and produced other upheavals. For instance, Jeremiah could have been in the car at the time it was set on fire BUT GOD prevented it. This could have caused him to be severely burned or even caused his death. Likewise, he could have seen the perpetrators and tried to take things into his own hands. This could have led to a physical altercation which could have ended in serious injuries or death, BUT GOD did not allow it. Therefore, there is so much to be thankful for despite the contemptible situation or offense. God always has a way to bring VICTORY and TRIUMPH in the midst of adversity. Another important note to share is although the car was virtually totally charred, it was protected by insurance. The insurance company completely paid the vehicle off, and Jeremiah was able to get another one. Consequently, we can plainly see that when the enemy comes to burn or destroy something in our lives God can or will intervene. He will come into our circumstances and leave us with a burning testimony of FAITH and CONFIDENCE in him.

"You intended to harm me, but God intended it for good to accomplish what is now being done, the saving of many lives." Genesis 50:20 (NIV)

Three Heart Attacks in One Year

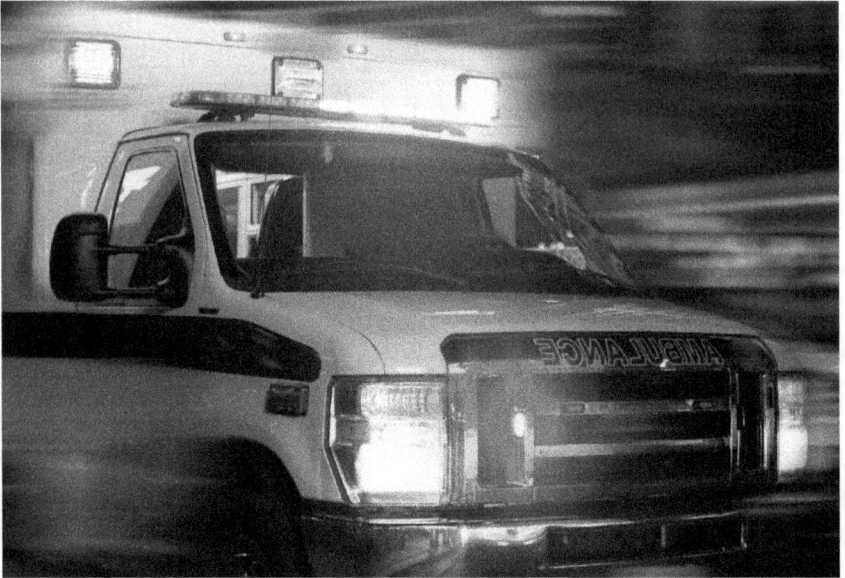

   April of 2014 was an unforgettable and life changing experience for Alex Heard and his family. He had enjoyed good health for eighty years and had worked as a police officer for a long time. In fact, he was still working in law enforcement at the ripe, delightful age of 80. He had made it his lifetime career, and it spanned over fifty years. Some would even say that he lived and breathed law enforcement! Frankly said, it was his life and he enjoyed it.

   April of that year would be a month that he and his wife, Linnie, lives' would be put in a tailspin. Nothing could have prepared him or his wife for the days, weeks, months, or even years ahead, But God. Without any warning, he suffered his first heart attack and was taken to the hospital. It was a frightening experience especially since he had never been gravely sick before. That day he found himself under the doctor's care for a very serious, life threatening condition. To those who loved him, the news felt like their breath was being cut off, and the thought of losing him was both piercing and unbearable to accept. However, there's something about the power of God's love and his grace. There is also something about a family and a church family praying for someone and calling their name out to God. I can say without any reservation that God responds to any sincere prayer on behalf of another human being. And, so he did in this situation.

He responded and granted mercy and grace to Alex Heard who is affectionately called Daddy, Dadknee, Pops, and Alex by those who knew him best. By God's grace, he escaped the thralls of death and was able to return home with medications. Expensive and strong medications that is! It was a time of true thanksgiving and gratefulness. Sadly, it would only be about two months before the enemy would strike again. When June rounded the corner, it brought with it even greater crushing blows. That month he had not one but two more heart attacks. The enemy was on a mission to take away both his health and his life. At eighty years old, how could he withstand two more heart attacks? But God. The second heart took place at home and the third one at the hospital. The news spread like wildfire. It was undoubtedly paralyzing and unnerving. Family members were bombarded with many fear filled thoughts and thoughts of uncertainty. The doctors at the hospital worked with him, and by God's grace he made it through the critical and crucial times. However, his heart was severely damaged and weak. It was now functioning at a very low level. But against the odds, he was blessed to leave the hospital and return to his home in about a week. The doctors did virtually all they could do for him besides prescribe medications. Their prognosis and life expectancy for him was highly unfavorable. In fact, when he showed up for appointments, they would be shocked that he was still alive. His testimony was, "I'm blessed." He always remembered to give God the glory for his life especially in his latter years. He was graced to live approximately eight more years. He maintained a grateful attitude, and he never missed an opportunity to teach or testify of God's wonderful goodness and his amazing grace. Even on his lowest days, he would say, "Honey, I'm blessed." God graced him to live through three heart attacks at age eighty, and he extended his life eight more years. This story lets us know that God is in favor of long life, and he honors the faith of any person at any age. He also honors prayers for people of any age. Just like he is not a respecter of persons, he is also not a respecter of age. Truly faith and prayer made the difference in his life and even the prolonging of his life. But God!

"Then he turned his face to the wall, and prayed unto the Lord...I will add fifteen years to his life" II Kings 20:2-6 (KJV)

Christina's Prayer

As a little girl, Christina was sensitive, unique, and beautiful in her own right. She was both loveable and peculiar. She spent a lot of time at her grandmother's house. Now her grandmother was a loving but firm woman having raised six children of her own. She was very candid and was careful to be understood when she spoke. In short, she was a woman that meant what she said, and said what she meant. She never seemed to leave a question mark as to what she was saying or what her expectations were. If by chance, you acted like you didn't understand she didn't mind helping you. She had a way of giving you a quick, meaningful lesson on "understanding."

She had a hand in most of her grandchildren's lives. Therefore, she expected them to get along and act like family. However, if you know anything about children, you know that they get into stuff. That is, they commit some mischievous and unthinkable acts, they get into scraps, tussles, and just plain old disagreements and fights.

One day Christina's cousin, Mark, and she got into it. You may say, they got into what. Well, they got into one of those plain old, ugly fights which was spoken about earlier. At that age, they were not wise enough to keep the situation low key, and boy that meant TROUBLE for them. Anyway, their grandmother, Delois, got wind of it, and needless to say, she was NOT happy. Their behavior caused her to speak her famous but dreadful words. She said, "I'm going to whip you!" Even to date, her own children still tell stories about those infamous words. When those words reached Christina's ears and registered in her mind, she was TERRIFIED! OH, BOY was she SCARED!!! Perhaps, at that moment, her thoughts went haywire, and all she could think about was how to escape. Perhaps, she said within herself, "How can I get away from grandmama? And, how can I get away from this WHIPPING?" She quickly sprang into action and ran out of the house. She ran to the small, white painted church across the street. She began circling it again and again. She was crying and praying at the top of her lungs. When she would make it to the front of the church, she would stop and pray. She prayed, "JESUS, PLEASE don't let Grandma whip me!" She continued to run, cry, and pray vehemently. Both her cries and her prayers drew the neighbors outside. At first, they wondered what was going on, and then they saw it. It was Christina running, crying, and praying! She was calling on the name of JESUS for help! She continued to do this for a while. Neighbors, spectators, and family members alike were beholding Christina's hysterical and dramatical cries and prayers. It became both touching and comical to all who witnessed it. It touched her grandmother so much that she decided NOT to whip her. All of Christina's beseeching, tears, and prayers won her grandmother over. She realized that what she needed that day was love, compassion, and understanding.

Christina, though a little girl, experienced God's intervention and compassion simply by praying that day. She knows all too well that she would have gotten a whipping, But God intervened on her behalf. Because he did, she missed feeling the painful stings of her grandmother's willow switches that day. This story lets us know that God is listening to our prayers, and he will intervene in any situation no matter your age or no matter what you have done.

"And he took them up in his arms, put his hands upon them, and blessed them." Mark 10:16 (KJV)

A Crazy Relationship

Have you ever endeavored to do the right thing only to find out way down the road that it wasn't so right? Or, shall we say, it wasn't so right for you? Well, this was the case and situation that Shae faced. Shae is a beautiful young lady with a mild temperament, loving, and has a contagious sense of humor. Like most young women she desired companionship and hoped to one day have her own family. One day she met someone who appeared to tick all the right boxes or so it seemed on the surface. She was cautious but in hindsight she realized that there had been some definite serious red flags. Red flags that she knows she should have taken heed to. Some of which she was willing to chop up to believing he would change over time. However, that's not always the case. After dating for a while, they took the plunge. With a few family members tuned into Zoom, they said, "I do." This was a marriage bred out of the Covid-19 pandemic or what some refer to as the Corona Virus pandemic.

Things went okay for a while, and they were enjoying the bliss of married life. Each one putting their best foot forward and putting on their best behavior. However, after a period of time, things began to unravel, and her husband began to flip. He simply started to change and change drastically! He started operating in a controlling manner. EVERYTHING had to be the way he wanted it. Or, EVERYTHING had to go just as he said or as he had planned. Anything that happened outside of his agenda or his plans would result in arguments, yelling's, and put downs. All of which equates to verbal and emotional abuse. Her spouse would often wake up picking fights and spitting out hostile anger! Nothing seemed to satisfy him. He would get enraged about the smallest thing and then use his ANGER and INTIMIDATION to try to force her to respond to his illogical rants and questions. He was bent on using any means to exercise control over her and make her engage in frivolous, meaningless, and futile arguments. Things got so bad she felt like she was walking on 'eggshells' so to speak. She found herself often thinking or saying to herself, "I better do this or not do that, cause I don't want him to get mad or upset." EVERYTHING became about him. So much so that she LOST herself and almost her sanity! The day to day mental anguish wore on her as an individual, as a woman, and as a human being. His words and constant badgering slowly ate away at her well-being, her peace, and her personage. There even came times in the relationship when the verbal fights or assaults wound up becoming physical. She was forced to defend herself and mind you, she is no push over. That being said, please know this, neither verbal abuse nor physical abuse is EVER okay. In dealing with him, whatever the case, whether verbal or physical, he would always manage to lay the blame at her feet. Never being able to take responsibility for his actions or behavior.

As the situation grew worse and worse, she found herself complaining and complaining about what was going on. Complaining in itself is not terrible, but if we're not careful, it can be like rocking in a rocking chair. We can end up doing the same thing and staying in the same position or situation. Consequently, nothing changes! Understandably, she was upset, devastated, and also, she started having anxiety attacks. Something definitely needed to change and quickly. Then she began to cry out to God saying, "Why did I have to end up with this person? Why am I going through this?" God, with his loving kindness, spoke to her heart and said, "You didn't consult me or involve me in your decision to marry this person." From that point on, she made the decision to stop complaining and start praying and reading the word of God more. She knew by doing this she would receive peace, and perhaps, she would get the answers she needed. Though the relationship was volatile, it pushed her into a place of intimacy with God, our Father. The cultivation of her relationship with God restored her peace, joy, self-worth, and SANITY. Since that time, they have both gone their separate ways, and the relationship has dissolved. Today, Shae thanks God for walking with her through her journey and teaching her the difference between 'so-called' love which breeds abuse, and real love which produces care, unselfishness, and peace.

"He brought me up also out of a horrible pit, out of the miry clay, and set my feet upon a rock and established my goings." Psalms 40:2 (KJV)

God Made the Difference

As Yvette grew up, there were many, many things she pondered. There were so many questions. She states, "Growing up I was made to feel like the black sheep of the family, and I never seemed to do anything right. I was made to feel like I was nothing and was often told I would never amount to anything. Even when I was assaulted as a child, the perpetrator would taunt me with the very same words." Imagine the pain, the sense of abandonment, the mental and sexual abuse she suffered through. Needless to say, this was a devastating, difficult, and challenging life for a little girl. But, where could she go and who could she turn to? She grew up basically without the constant presence of her parents. Consequently, she was brought up by her grandparents and later by her great grandparents. At the time of both her conception and birth, her biological parents were very, very young and naive. Neither of them was ready nor equipped to be parents. So, they went on with their lives and lived it on their own terms. Simply put, they were just out there living life as teenagers. They were young, far from being mature, and just not ready to shoulder the responsibility of a child. That's not to say that they didn't love Yvette because they did, but a lack of their presence definitely put an awful hole in her soul. As a child, she wrestled with the fact that they were not really in her life. She just didn't understand why they weren't there. She thought and said many times inwardly, "What is wrong with me?" "What have I done to cause them not to be here with me or for me?" Therefore, her life was filled with a lot of questions which opened the door for both abandonment and rejection.

As a result of feeling both abandoned and rejected, Yvette developed a deep, deep desire or longing to be loved and to be accepted. Hurt, broken, and dejected she needed something, or she needed someone to fill the void and emptiness. The sense of true belongingness, affirmation, and acceptance had escaped her even as a young child. Her innocence was viciously ripped away from her. She desperately needed these intangibles, and she definitely wanted them. So, she searched diligently for them, but no matter how hard she looked for them, she always came up empty. This was because she searched for them in all the wrong places. She searched for them in alcohol trying to fit in with those around her. She clung to the false hope of receiving their love and acceptance in return. However, every single time she came up empty. She searched for them through illicit relationships. However, each one proved to be fruitless and nothing but let downs. They never yielded the love, acceptance, affirmations that she so desperately needed or wanted. Instead, there were disappointments after disappointments. Nothing seemed to work out despite her outward beauty, physique, and status.

After the unsuccessful attempts and pitfalls in relationships, she came to a place that she no longer wanted to live. Her emotions were spent, her mind clouded, and her heart was broken in so many pieces. Thoughts of not wanting to live and not being necessary flooded her mind. The enemy did what he could to push her OVER the EDGE. The time came when she did the unthinkable in trying to end her life. Sadly, this happened more than once. She was tired of hurting! She was tired of being rejected! She was tired of feeling like she was nothing! She wanted to end it all because she thought committing suicide was the way out. However, God with his great love intervened, and he spared her life.

Today, though she still has questions, she has turned to The Almighty God for understanding and strength. She knows that he is truly the answer, and that she is truly loved and accepted by him. As she looks over her life, she knows that God has made all the difference and has given her a life worth living. He has opened her eyes to his love and genuine care for her. He is a faithful and loving Father that will continue to walk this journey of life with her.

"To the roots of the mountains I sank down; the earth beneath barred me in forever. But you, LORD my God, brought my life from the pit." Jonah 2:6 (NIV)

Fighting for My Life

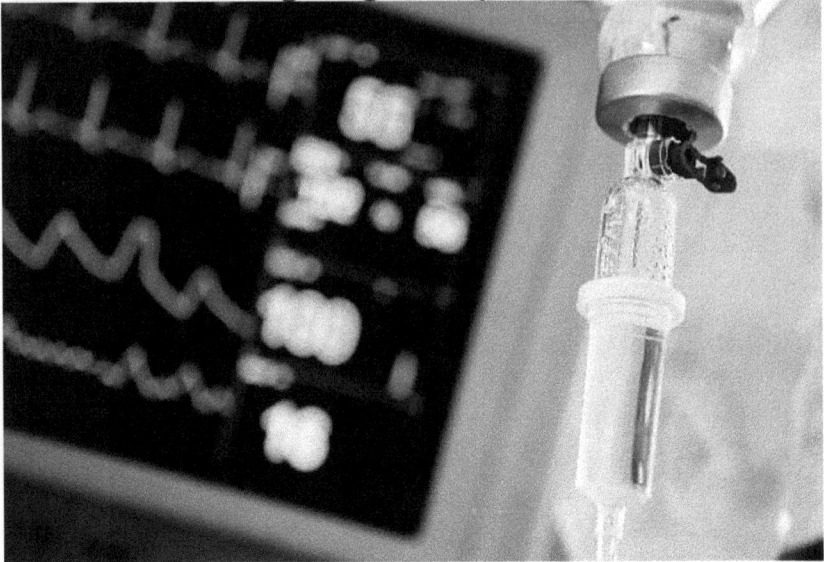

Simmie Jr. is a very well-known musician. He has loved music and in particular, the drums for many, many years. He has been passionate about them since his youth and has worked over the decades to perfect and hone his skills. He has been graced to travel throughout the country and meet some of the most renowned gospel singers. For example, Tim Rogers, Donnie McClurkin, and Rance Allen. Some of his travels and performances have been in states such as Georgia, Arizona, Texas, New Jersey, as well as many others. Some of the groups that he has played with are the Disciples, True Believers, Tim Rogers, along with other groups over the course of many years. Music is undoubtedly his love! It is a vital part of his life! He pours his soul into playing his favorite instrument. It is his way of expressing his deeper inner self and his form of worship to God. Playing the drums is his ministry to God. It is a language he speaks not only to his listeners, but most importantly to God, his maker.

During his travels down through the years, he has been fortunate to enjoy doing what he loves. While many people live most of their lives working at what they hate or really don't care for, he has been graced to do his passion. Along with being blessed to do what he loves, he has also enjoyed the blessing of good to reasonable health. However, in 2023, he was blindsided by some serious medical problems. Some that went from bad to worse and from tolerable to intolerable. Something that had once been a small problem and had presented minor discomfort spiraled into something unimaginable. He was doing fine and feeling ok the day before, but something happened the next day that took him totally by surprise. He began to feel sick like he had never experienced before. Consequently, he was taken to the hospital. Upon arrival, they took his vital signs, and they also ran a series of tests. His blood pressure was out of whack and extremely high. The doctors found it very difficult and challenging to get it stabilized. It was a continuous battle for a period of time, and it posed an immediate threat to both his life and to his health. This was particularly alarming and confusing because he had never suffered from hypertension before. Not only did his blood pressure pose a remarkable problem, but his calcium level was also highly elevated. The reason for its elevation still remains a mystery to date. Thankfully, the doctors were eventually able to do a procedure to stabilize it. That was definitely a much needed victory. Nevertheless, they were still facing the initial problem with his gallbladder. For some reason, it was inflamed and irritated. It was believed that it was causing all the other problems throughout his body. The doctors wanted to remove it, but they were hindered because of the various elevations he was experiencing. However, they did decide to insert tubes into his body to drain fluids and toxins from his gallbladder. With all of these medical complications going on, Simmie Jr. found himself in the Intensive Care Unit (ICU) trusting God. A place that he had no plans to be, it was very surreal! He shared with his wife, Brittney, while he was in there God revealed to him that he wanted him to have a deeper relationship with him. He also shared that he had a "behind the veil" experience with God in ICU. It was also in that place that he and his wife decided on this motto: "Strong Finish, Strong Faith." When he was in ICU, they monitored his vital signs intensely, gave medications, and ran IVs. Of course, they also continued with both testing and observations. His body was undergoing a lot of changes and a lot of trauma. Things looked grim for a while. Both his family and friends continued in prayer on his behalf, and two of his cousins, Hope and Christina, came to visit and pray for him when he was hospitalized the first time. Seeing them seemed to lift his spirits and add another dose of hope and courage. The doctors continued to work with him and after a while, he was able to go home. Not long afterwards, his dad, Simmie Sr., came to visit and spend some time with him and help with his care. It's a time that neither of them will ever forget and will always cherish.

In spite of being able to return home, for some reason, he was not able to eat or drink. When he attempted to do either, it would just come right back up. This went on for weeks at a time and even progressed into months. He lost a tremendous amount of weight, approximately eighty pounds. Without sustained nutrition, he was becoming weaker and weaker. Even his voice began to weaken and became very frail. He was slowly slipping away with nothing of nutritional value sticking or staying in his body. At some point, he became UNRESPONSIVE, and ended up going back into the hospital desperately needing a true remedy or resolve for this situation. His father and his cousin came back to Mississippi to see him from Oklahoma. His family covered him with a blanket of prayer upon hearing the news of his condition. They knew that the Almighty God was the answer and the healer. Their prayers were accompanied by a host of many, many friends, acquaintances, his wife, and his church family as well. Finally, to address this critical problem, the doctors did what was needed to stabilize him. One of the many things they also did put in a feeding tube so that his body could receive necessary nourishment. Also to keep his body from shutting down. This was indeed great news! After that procedure, he was alert and talking like nothing had happened, but the journey and recovery was an uphill battle.

Today Simmie Jr. is continuing to progress. His voice is becoming stronger, and he has regained some much needed weight. However, he is still fighting for both his health and his life. But God! Every day is a fight, but he knows he can win because he is fighting the GOOD FIGHT of FAITH. Though this has been a long and intense journey for him, his wife, and his family, he knows that God is FAITHFUL. He also knows he will see him through. When asked how her husband's sickness has affected her, Brittney said, "It has helped me to see who people really are." She shared that she felt people had let them down especially when they needed financial help. Despite the letdown, they know God has been a constant presence in their journey, and he has provided for their every need. He is still on the throne and deserves the glory for his prevailing power, mercy, and provision during such a trying and challenging time.

"For indeed he was sick nigh unto death: but God had mercy on him; and not on him only, but on me also, lest I should have sorrow upon sorrow." Philippians 2:27 (KJV)

The Case of the Missing Wallet

Everyone has had an occasion to misplace something. Perhaps we have misplaced our car keys, an important document, or even an appointment card. When it happens, we usually go through our usual self-rebuke and expression of frustration. That is, frustration with ourselves because we know we should have paid better attention to where we were laying or putting things down. Sometimes we go through the phase of regret and anguish knowing that if we were just ORGANIZED, this or that wouldn't have happened again. Or, we may even think if we were just ORGANIZED we could have found what we needed and been on time for a particular appointment. Yet, we find ourselves laboring under the same unfulfilled promise we have made to ourselves countless times before. The promise is simply this, "I'm going to get organized and stay organized. I'm going to put things in their proper place and keep them in their proper place." Though organization is indeed innate for some, many others find it to be a lofty goal which sometimes seems unattainable, but so very necessary. Yes necessary! Why? Because when we are organized, it makes our lives more peaceful and things absolutely flow much, much better. We also walk with a sense of confidence because we have taken the time to rid ourselves of the chaos, frustration, and undermining yoke that disorganization brings. However, organization is definitely key, no one needs to feel condemned because we all have been guilty of misplacing something. Even the most organized person has had occasion to put something in the wrong place or just plain misplace something. It's just a part of our humanness.

Dealing with the hustle and bustle of life many times leaves us doing things involuntarily. That is to say, we do a lot of things without putting direct focus or attention on what we're doing. This means in most of our day to day dealings we operate without keen or precise focus. Consequently, we find ourselves doing the same things and winding up with the same results. We lay things down in unestablished places, and then we rant and rave because we can't find them. How hilarious! And, who can we blame, but ourselves? Yes, that person in the mirror is usually the one who is to blame. In some cases, it's not just unimportant things that we just simply lay around or lay down. NO!!! Sometimes they are indeed vital things or things that we need on a daily basis. There again we promise ourselves that we are going to do better. We make self-promises that we are going to get organized and stay ORGANIZED! However, in most cases, we only land right back into the same old habits and routines. We find ourselves laying things down anywhere and everywhere again and again. Laying things down here and there. Laying things down on any available or convenient surface. How funny! On the other hand, not so funny because it can become a dreadful, frustrating, and self-defeating cycle. But the good is, it can be changed by God's miraculous intervention. When we come to the end of ourselves and our frustrations, we usually look to him. Yes, we look up. Amazingly, he cares about every part of our lives. He will get involved if we humble ourselves and ask him to. Let's see how he got involved in something as simple, yet profound as a wallet.

One day Emmanuel discovered that he no longer had his wallet. He had unknowingly misplaced it. The question was where? He, like others, carried a lot of important things in his wallet. Things like his driver's license, social security card, bank and credit cards. His passport was also in it along with other important documents. Initially, he didn't think much about it. He knew it should have been in a familiar place. Perhaps, in his house or in his vehicle would have been the most likely places he thought. Therefore, he wasn't alarmed or really concerned. He was sure it would turn up. He mentioned it to his wife, Fithawit, and she hadn't seen it or put it up for him. So, he went through each day wondering and looking here and there for it. However, it did not turn up. Time went on and still no wallet. Then approaching two weeks of its disappearance, the necessity to find it arose. In fact, it was imperative that he find it. He needed to use a card in the wallet to complete an important project. It then became an urgent matter. He started looking for it again. He looked in almost every room in the house again. He looked in and, on his couches, and still came up empty. He also looked in his vehicles. He looked in the seats, under the seats, and between the seats. He looked in the glove compartment and on the floor all to no avail. He thought, "Where in the world could it be?" He further thought, "Did Fithawit hide it or put it up and just forgot?" So, he asked his wife again, "Did you see or move my wallet?" Her answer was a firm but loving, "No!" Afterwards he called his mother and asked if he had left it over to their house. Her reply also was, "No." When she found this out, she began to pray about it. Without a doubt, this situation was becoming increasingly FRUSTRATING. By now, time was pressing, and he needed to find it immediately to complete the project. So, his search continued. He mulled it over and over in his mind. He searched the places he had searched previously. He even went to Walmart to see if he had left it there and then to another store. However, the trips to the stores proved to be futile because the answer again was no! He was frustrated to say the least, but finally he called his brother, Jeremiah. He came over to his house to help him search for the wallet. They searched several places and then they went back into the den which he calls his "man cave." They focused on the couch again. They looked on one side of the couch and felt between the cushions, and in the back of them. Still nothing. Then his brother decided to take a look at the other part of the sectional couch which Emmanuel rarely ever uses. He lifted it up, and what did he see? It was the MISSING WALLET! The ELUSIVE wallet was revealed! Of course, Emmanuel immediately said, "I found it," being both comical and facetious. They both let out a deep, hearty laugh. However, they realize that in the end, or at the end of the day the wallet was found because of persistence, prayer, and help from his brother. These were the components that solved the case of the missing wallet. Consequently, he was able to complete his business project while giving The Most High praise for his intervention.

"Ask, and it shall be given you; seek, and ye shall find; knock, and it shall be given you." Matthew 7:7 (KJV)

A Walking Time Bomb!

We have heard of different types of bombs such as the atomic bomb, nuclear bomb, or even pipe bombs. Though, each is made of different materials or properties, they each have the very same ability and purpose. That ability and purpose is to kill, to destroy, or to maim. In other words, they are never formed or made or sent forth to preserve human life or anything else in its pathway. Their mission is for the demise of one's life or purpose, and subsequently anything else that they come in contact with. As we think of different types of bombs, let's consider the following question. The question is, have you ever heard of "A Walking Time Bomb?" Yes, "A WALKING TIME BOMB!" You see, sometimes we as humans can have unknown or unrealized medical issues festering in our bodies. They may lie dormant or give us no cause for alarm for weeks, months, or even years. We may trudge through life doing our day to day activities and taking care of business, none the wiser. While inside of our bodies, something so frightening and life threatening is about to turn our lives upside down. That something can be so treacherous and so dangerous that it can warrant being called or compared to a WALKING TIME BOMB. It may be high blood pressure which is often called the silent killer. It can be high or elevated cholesterol which can lead to heart attacks or heart disease. It can be blood clots that are ready to invade various parts of the body which can lead to amputation, stroke, or even an aneurysm. Lastly, it can also be a tubal pregnancy which can be fatal if not properly diagnosed and properly dealt with in a timely manner. (A tubal pregnancy occurs 90% of the time in the fallopian tube. As a pregnancy grows, it can cause the tube to burst (rupture). A rupture can cause internal bleeding and become a life threatening emergency). So, you see any serious medical condition can be or cause you to become a "WALKING TIME BOMB!" So, it was with Winifred. Let's see how God intervened in her life in the early 1980's.

For about two weeks, Winifred had been experiencing pain in the lower part of her stomach. She had gone to a military doctor at least two times. The doctor had given her medication for what he had determined to be a urinary tract infection. After going to him the second time, the pain and discomfort only INTENSIFIED. The pain was sharp and felt like contractions. They progressed and progressed. They got sharper and sharper. The pain worsened to the degree that all she could do was just lay on the couch. She laid there hoping the medication would work and the pain would subside. But, unfortunately, it didn't. It Persisted! Eventually, her mother (Delois) said to her before going out of town, "You need to go back to the doctor." Winifred took her advice and made another appointment. This time she went to a civilian doctor. In fact, he was her longtime primary care doctor. She went to the appointment, and the doctor took tests and did an exam. The results were quite alarming and immediately he went into action. She was instantly sent to the emergency room to be admitted to the hospital and scheduled for emergency surgery! She had a tubal pregnancy and the doctor said to her, "You are a WALKING TIME BOMB! You could rupture ANY MINUTE!" She was shocked and felt INCREDIBLE FEAR understandably! When asked if she was scared, her reply was, "YES." She said, "I was scared mostly because I was alone." Yes, this untimely medical emergency happened at the same time that her mother, her children, and one of her sisters were out of town, BUT GOD was there. She went into surgery alone yet NOT alone. God guided the doctor's hands that day. Thanks to him, she had made it just in the nick of time, and the surgery was successful.

This can be a lesson to us all. When we feel uneasiness or pain, let's not be so quick to dismiss it or put off going to seek medical help. Our bodies are designed to respond to abnormalities and distress. It sends us messages and sometimes warnings through both uneasiness and pain. Let's learn to be sensitive to it. Listen to it. Honor it. It may very well save our lives one day and keep us from being or becoming a 'WALKING TIME BOMB!'

"I shall not die, but live, and declare the works of the Lord" Psalms 118:17 (KJV)

www.ingramcontent.com/pod-product-compliance
Lightning Source LLC
Chambersburg PA
CBHW052214090426
42741CB00010B/2537